*Praise for*

# STRANGE BEACH

"The poems in *Strange Beach* are as sure in their storytelling as centuries-old myths. These poems explain the world to me, rebuild it in front of my eyes with polysensory images that don't stop moving."

—TAYLOR BYAS, author of *I Done Clicked My Heels Three Times*, winner of the Maya Angelou Book Award

"In this exciting debut, the tide line of the poetic phrase is constantly shifting, is forever rebuilt and remade on the sands of language, every grain of a word held up to the light to consider its myriad refractions."

—ANDREW MCMILLAN, author of *Pity*

# STRANGE BEACH

SOFT SKULL ✶ NEW YORK

# STRANGE BEACH

POEMS

OLUWASEUN OLAYIWOLA

STRANGE BEACH

First Soft Skull edition: 2024

Grateful acknowledgment for reprinting materials is made to the following: Claudia Rankine, excerpt from ["Listen, you,"] from *Citizen: An American Lyric*. Copyright © 2014 by Claudia Rankine. Reprinted with the permission of The Permissions Company, LLC, on behalf of Graywolf Press.

Library of Congress Cataloging-in-Publication Data
Names: Olayiwola, Oluwaseun, author.
Title: Strange beach : poems / Oluwaseun Olayiwola.
Other titles: Strange beach (Compilation)
Description: First Soft Skull edition. | New York : Soft Skull, 2025.
Identifiers: LCCN 2024039399 | ISBN 9781593767761 (trade paperback) |
    ISBN 9781593767778 (ebook)
Subjects: LCGFT: Poetry.
Classification: LCC PR6115.L25 S77 2025 | DDC 821/.92—dc23/eng/20240830
LC record available at https://lccn.loc.gov/2024039399

*Cover design and illustration by Victoria Maxfield*
*Book design by tracy danes*

Soft Skull Press
New York, NY
www.softskull.com

Printed in the United States of America
10  9  8  7  6  5  4  3  2  1

*for Miray Mehmet Fontanelli*

# Contents

●——●

●——●

●——●

## Strange Beach

—unable to get from the underneath side of
                the stones
                that flank the sand, the body: blown

from every direction into, like a conch shell

where the echo of emotion    in extremis    floods

                the chamber

where once was a body willing to die inside of, longing—this
        is the obsession, this transatlantic voyage
        spread on the page
                like an oil spill, the blue-and-black

arsenal of water hushing, inevitably: *was it worth it?*

        Worth. It circles around you—

the increasing gap between the surface
                of the water
                and the stillness you entirely inhabit

so as to sink to the ocean floor: but properly
with no effect on velocity. Stingrays.

Desire: inseparability of light
        and dark. How beautiful

you have been and are

        giving your whole life to a pointless competition—

No, it's a strange beach; each body is a strange beach, and if you let in the excess emotion you will recall the Atlantic Ocean breaking on our heads.

CLAUDIA RANKINE, *Citizen*

## More Night

In the Book of Unusable Minutes,
        the passengers like skyward lights.
Sun lifting his broken arms
        like a dying thing, the burning center
moving along time's cargo,
        archaic gauze, each
perpendicularity a mazed
        patchwork of veins
where healing had words
        to unpick and kept its mouth
shut, a genteel child in the cabin—

Long haul. Year of trillions
        and the plane soaring
into its wilding airscape, the farther-out
        distances of carbon—Is
this my airborne home I cannot
        outrun. These, our eyes
focusing downward
        where God is just
this once, yes, the origin
        of interiority from our lungs

starting blank weather and do you
        hear it? The ears
in our chests? The past in each of us
        blistering, chapping,
the pus arriving like snow,
        sleepwalker of indecision—What do
we declare for small things,
        the hydraulic weight of being
looked at, deliberately, persistently—

Then the durational string-pluck
          of turbulence shearing prayer
from the body's tarmac, the unpacking
          like an era that refuses to end or begin again.
*Here, have more night*
          the mind says. And as if from nowhere,
*Here, have more blue,*
          Are you feeling too simple?
Are you wanting the glazed
          lake of memory to shoot up
for air and take
          more of you back with it
when it goes?

Faces with wishes stitched across them
          like large quilts.
And the sunset, even from this high up,
          tips down along the dark
outcome of sky. Immeasurable beauty
          is immeasurable precisely
until it's gone—

## Simulacrum

There wasn't love but there was what love becomes—

(sheet-wrinkle)(skin-dune)(arm-ropes lassoing

our neck flesh with push-and-pull—, equal amounts;

the hurt convincing its shape is false, the relation:

the recorded moment (he likes to record) not true)—

Then the film buffering . . . the unfinished triangle

your body sculpts on top of his.

Frustration. Yes. Rejection. Oh yes.

The colon's ring hammering, waking up (*not again, not*

*tonight*). Tight. Loose. Bloodless (for now), dragging

a palm across the brick wall—now

blood (for now) streaming from you like scripture—:

spit of him landing atop your eyelid, that puddled need.

And there is freedom, there is intention to break your back in half

and call it *what-you-asked-for*, what your separateness

will not allow. Rattle of wooden slats (indentations

in the linen), this body you are finally inside of

being molded into the cushion's canvas

by what desire has given him permittance to do tonight, tonight only—


He is not a perfect fit and that is perfect. He will not

stay the night. He will not stay. Hard

night. Leaking night. No fine point, needled stars.

The sky is a masculinity. He starts the car.

Likes to be called daddy. Needs to be called

something, anything.

There is your obligation, your obliging. Call it

gratitude. Be

grateful. Give

thanks. Give.

## Animal Song

The country lights are real upon the stampede of pigs that fuss
and bisect around an obstacle of straw.
Grass, newly cut, holds the pettitoes' rushed
imprint, doesn't let go, cannot fetch as the pigs
split themselves on (choice entering with a dirt
finish, odorous, rank) a scarecrow in a field.

Where he's been sewn up, as in repaired, I can see it.
Stacked lesions in his back that with training
vertically thread a new spine, the underwritten narrative
of sun setting over the pigs' unified face. Collectivity.
Wish. Throw. Brightness. And yet it takes a dark
to know a dark. Unquantifiable quickness.

There are those we let have sway over us.
There are those who innately have it—There. Go.
With your feet. Into the designated pen. I can follow
and be quiet. Weakening, then truly weakened.

How many steps between rest and defeat until the flame
is what it always was: a symbol
for where the slaughter ends. Red-blue pool
of drained life swirling
under, refusing purple, refusing memory's
tainted leakage—And passing through
the body like an event. When does it become
trespass? It's Tuesday. He is coming
over to demonstrate squirm's meaning: to writhe inside
the self. How even the bones tangle, country light
fading the room at the same angle
we had thought it departed—

## Fumbled Sonnet

Ocean—though from below
you can't quite tell; below,
not in it. What's the saying? It is impossible
to be on the outside
of your situation the way cure
is yoked like a blue ember
to diagnosis—Okay,
I'll say it: the new lover
must fuck the old one
out of memory. Pressure, point
of contact, all this
they decide, though speed
is of the utmost
importance when it comes to
time's bold effects: heaven
of the body smudged like a ghost
losing its yell because it gets one more day
as matter on earth—what would you say
differently if that thing
you thought was dead
could matter once more? Brightly,
the blade's luster blinds
whom it has decided
to renovate; you
know nothing about the
feeling but that your abdomen
is, after all this thinking, bleeding,
swelling with blue light—

## The Mark

and having been        cast away (different
                                              to being thrown
                    out of the light) by wind
                                        though what truly
these days is the difference
                    when the body is
                            lawlike, always involved        when
the scatteredness grief makes of devotion
                                                        lies before you
                        like a stupid adjective
rolling in the grass: inevitable
                    is the way any swinging        thing
finds rest: (as in        what we                ought
                            to do
                    after being fought
        into parenthood; what we
                        leave behind) at the bottom—a violent
fire-dream hollowing out the seen-through-to space

behind the eyes
            like a tattoo. My mother                forbade us
                            from bringing any

permanent mark        to our skin—Son;
            crack in the wall.

My mother had visions
                    I think
                            with grace and
            aplomb
is how I stole them—

## My Mother Raised a Normal Man

Then me.

•———•

Any normal man cuts violations to his hairline.
A master of bodily function, say, a sculptor.

To his hairline he articulates: you will be exact.
And, if not exact, an enemy.

•———•

At the barbershop I'm silent.
Plenty of shoptalk: sports, women,
women as sports.

When I join in
they can tell I can tell
I'm a fake.

I remind them of their girlfriends. The way I enunciate,
always offering manifold angles on narrative—
us girlfriends, both protagonist
and foil.

My mother's voice in my head: Don't
embarrass me. Don't
embarrass God.

Such power. To throw God into doubt,
a rolled-up tangle of dead follicles
thrown to sky.

I let my boyfriend pull my hair out
when we fuck. It's that good.

Counterintuitive, the scalp
is sensitive, I forget
I'm being split at the back end of a portal.

Him? His hair is silver.
When I touch his head, I divine the future
even though both our minds are empty
crystal balls.

Don't embarrass me. Don't embarrass God.
Embarrassment. I'm like
a black son. I'm bundling my hair
into a ponytail as we speak.

Five years since I cut my hair—
It's like a lover by now:
full of leaving.

When we're done we sit on opposite edges of the bed,
back-to-back like agitprop
depicting politicians as equal.

My hair's littered in the carpet like crumbs.

He faces the wall. I face his desk.
There stands a framed picture of him

and his ex, who was black, who was bald.

## Chlorine

I.

You, all laughs,

all jinglejangle,

closing the door, making riot

of a new text from an old friend.

I stared, as research, at the floor, carpeted

with strained arguments. Metaphysics.

Performativity. Translation. Joan Didion.

Your friend intended to type bigger.

But she sent nigger.

Autocorrect.

O Apple.

Ha ha ha. Haze.

What did you say?

       Ha ha ha. She typed n——

       Haze.

What did you say?

My breath running wingless.
Desire's questions waiting

like clocks without markers.
Cerulean love:

I thought it was this and it was.

The early paradise
of subjection. The scene, the unchosen
drapes of bone stripping the white

under white, the white
          under black/brown.

          Loudnesses I didn't hear.

The soul fissuring
          that wants to be summarized,
                    to be remembered as intangible

therefore fragile, an
inverted balloon,
or encrusted with the hard stone of dailiness,
weak at the knees like theory.


    II.

Days earlier, George Floyd.
We wanted to protest.
We didn't.
You were ill.

I excused it.
You came
home laughing.
I excused it.
Perspective ran its tap.
We were
unrecommendable, were
just media, actors
whom history
worked through
its writer's block with—
I loved you. I excused it.
My vision was blurry.
My contacts were in
too long, too long.
I ran out. The cost
of being visible
is being visible.

## There is nothing like that black voice!

is what he said
        after losing
the singing competition, he reckoned
        him and I have (nothing
serious) among
        his friends one
wine-drunken street
        in the Florentine night
his voice, very beautiful very
        Italian, operatic, the whole
history of smoke latching
        promise to his audition
generations of cigarettes
        straining
faces in the stones
        we walk over
my throat shovels open: O
        American theater
lowering over us
        like the past. Unanimously
I eat his friends'
        applause.

        There is nothing like that
black voice! he said
        not knowing there is
nothing like that
        I could voice back
that wouldn't change
        the temperature

## Beacon

In the end, the lighthouse
we had walked to
was never the point, being
only what we were
to the sea: blank moons
inside us, waxed,
astonished, slipped
like exposed oysters
down our throats.
That force. Those frozen
purple lips releasing
struggles of breath—fogging.
We climbed a ladder to the top
because there were no stairs

# Cruise

Because in the bushes we know desire is wrongly
    and often named wind

The birds stay away from here
   the ashy skin of the train tracks, leading us into one another like
    a storm

approaching the gut—three seconds
        they say, it takes to decide whether he is

    *an* animal or *my* animal

    for the duration of our reservation of touch
we share in the thicket

   of used condoms consecrating our want
   to be empty as ghosts, disheveled

of intellect, this heavy weaponry
a calm thought before the million flickerings
   like sand sprayed-up by sudden sea change. I stand

outside myself at the dune-peak
   like a god, without intention to intervene, to interweave,
    watching

    old sunglassed Portuguese men mill and thrust back
  names they've never known but idolize,

the sky disassembling itself into discretions
   as he
     (yes him)
       clothed in sunburn, waves me over

to his grotto

wanting to make of my body
        a haunt, a place he can step into now
        and never again as someone wholly sentient—

o dark lightning of pleasure zapping us into instance, o bigmindedness,
flitting the current as in *now*,

where is the way in? where is the man
who found slumber on the tree cradling
                                his penis like treasure.
I had I swear just seen him discarding
            the sacred; hard memory,

bouquets of rubber rabbitbrush, dirty and dry
baby wipes, sand, shit
drawing sand into clumps and back out again as the tide muddies.

                    Is that what they say?
                                Are we an error of biology

or to it? What is natural. What is reason. What alive. Crickets
        tossing up smooth syllables between the soundtracks

of parting. Sensation. Be enough.

## Coast

*Calm*, he said, in another language
I had become proficient in pretending
I understood. The beach was still
the beach: picturesque, cold
this time of year when everyone preferred
the closeness of coffee shops. *Need it be that serious? Yes,*
he said, the waves moaning how they're
moon-trained all year regardless of season,
folding, unfolding, unconcerned with us,
little interruptions in the way of things.

## Fate

There's a man
                in a brownstone
by a green; field

or not field;
                strained meadow
more likely, blue

blossoms tipping up
                like countrymen
gone to a war

they were not briefed on—
                still fight, defend,
absolution of light

                a uniform
differentiating
                what's in

from what's out:
                purity? filth?
Whoever decides

cannot spell his name
                in piss across
the other; drips

of an internal
                bile-yellow pool
draining his knees

beneath: I guess
   there's a triumph
in staying alive

long enough
   to answer questions
about fate—gravity

the bend downward,
   the resistance to bend
downward, the blueblossoms'

lapels forming
   a shield, a room,
nature containing

them as if
   all along
they had a say

in the shut matter.
   Close your eyes,
Beloved. How else

will you see
   what I will do
in you?

## Strange Beach

I pretend I can see them,
        the disappearances,
the transparent doors. No
        one notices. Or
everyone
has noticed already,
        the shadow-green
uptwists of bear's breeches

through the earth, upside
        down, the white
willow's
leaves incandescent, arcing
        to the ground their
chlorophyll techniques
        of low-wind
forgetting,
their shuffling, light:
darkness

we cannot look away from,
        every degree of day
casting
gleam's ache, down here,
over
        the sanded world—

If only I could take you
        there, into time's
perfectly
withered manipulations,
        into the river's black-
breath

unfolding its rope between
        vision's keylock
and the plumes of
delinquent
        smoke so swelled
they are by-now simply

air. The white willows struck
long
        after the rain cedes—I
tug a leaf from the branch,
        witness a new one
already growing in its place.
        Who could call this
beauty.
The filling-in of loss,
        like a mound of
edematous
leaf rot, keeping us
inconsolable
        and alive—

Do not touch me now
        —unless you
mean me
to open, open farther than
        this beach and what
we endured here, has
already
        opened me—Is it that
you think

I'd rather be anything else,
      that we were gifted
the option to be anything
      more, than
temporary.

## re: God


To you I bow down my thousand tongues, confess
the shadowed case of my mind, some would call this
a lie; some just living, and still some, necessary
to heaven, its sacred, swollen balloon-edge—how
would you know otherwise who
to send to hell, who
forgets their demons like an old telephone number—
I did my time, hallowed my attention. In church
I lifted my artery of repentance like boys
conditioned to believe singing was solely
an expulsionary practice. In giving praise
you could not return, my mouth blistered
into locusts, every dark orifice turning
into mirrors for worship.
It is in this self-sufficiency I can admit, disabused
of symbol—your preferred medium—I do
love you. But men: Are we not your image?
Isn't the sword preening upward from his pelvis
the only tactic of sweet fellowship you've left us?
Here I declare your counsel, you for whom
declarations of any sort are mere as children
following loose kites into stopless winds—

## Once

What scatters shipward in the water are the missable bodies,
        buoyant, litter-equivalent, their compasses
        pointing back to shore, opening
black-handed waves

in the reducible, nightmared ocean. Nightmares—
        does the ocean have them? From now on,
        the weather-shadowed seabirds
landing, digging their feet into these glimmer-faded islands

whose rot gives way to obedient foams. Freedom
        and memory: which sky empties into which

sky? This side of the atmosphere, do not call it space
        or time. More like irony, that brief

and grieving rhyme, that grief's aftereffect
        is its first effect, the seabirds

picking and folding, pick and fold, magnetized on the flotsam
        by what in their minds must mean

survival—a flare gun fires its last noun of *here-I-am*, sending birds
        abyssward and me, running back

through hedges of what had brought them
        to this blue maneuver of dream: to be inside

flight, to be damaged beyond the instinct of return——

## Greek Lesson After Anal

Once, a hookup described me as a siren
luring him out to the ocean.

Odysseus, Odysseus, sang the sirens,
though what they really meant was leave
your ejaculate everywhere
but where you target.

He had the characters accurate
but misunderstood the vector
of the dilemma. The sirens' beauty was to charm
consciousness out from Odysseus,
that he would cross
the bottomless sparkling pool
he thought was pleasure, consciousness
an underground fetish
rough sex can temporarily abate.

Also: drugs. Also: crowds.

If Odysseus was diligent,
he could have an orgy
of all three. What man,
in his right mind, wouldn't?

Then again, however much fucking
can seem to intimate
returning home inside another man,
we were not men.

## Nymphs

Everything was haze,
apparition, was left
behind, was idea, dried.
Was idea, after drying,
salvageable? I tell love
leave the cicadas—
dewy, segmented, jumpless—
to chirp invisibly from their joints
like species, define their mazes
of bone, define crunch, their
emerald notes like potato chips
crumbling down through
charred branches—Now
here the *I* comes,
swollen with hierarchy,
taken-down creatures, invested
infestations, no longer at
the triangle's summit
that gave us God,
gave us Destiny—
in the humanities
there's a saying:
what makes humans
exceptional is we withdraw
from the world.
The truth is a partial
painting. I bid you
withdraw, withdraw—

now you're back,
tell me, where
did you go
with all this oil

rinsing you
so you could not
stand in one place
and ask, *what,*
*what do I have*
*to celebrate?*

## The Kept Secret

It wasn't a mistake. Two Pomeranians
had been let in
the high grass, near me,

their faces sniffing,
wanting
to play catch with a third

buried friend, vanished
room of the living.
The *would-be-made-of* halting, the moment

occurring naturally
through you,
the bright light of the nose, again,

as if to guide them, the North
Star's illusion, going
toward what you seek. Over and over,

I wanted to say *yield, yield*, to bark
the comfort, the branched,
rooted wall mortality is: foliaged,

pocked with holes and
ruin. Dead dog in the garden:
I should have seen it
but what is wonder? And does it

go extinct? Helplessness
like a game of cards. And
what the living do when they happen, the

overgrown putrescence that must come differently,
the mind's woods
in which the trees rise out of habit

as figures upturned—

## Poem

You weren't invited to winter.

You showed up anyway,
asphalt weights around your wrists.

You took risks, you defined mercy
as survival, keeping the tested traditions
of your mother alive.

In reality she is not dead
but writing is, at best, protest.
Not protection.

You want to see to the end of the world,
you want a heartbeat of smoke
to pursue you like a voice
charmed out
by the universe's brass instrument,

want to think being swelled by tenor, by the soft lacquer
of beginnings, is to be safe from rust,
from necessary, because promised, wear.

Things for which there is
no technique
of preservation long enough—

It is not just your soul floundering
for permanence. The leaves are old crowns
rejecting the cobblestone
they are framed inside.

What will you do when they clear out?
What will you do when they are all but cleared out?

**Ski**

Descent

Snow, down the incline,
quick slalom, quicker
to be exhausted,

goggles on the face
blocking ice,
constellations

up above, thick
birds, fluttering
starlight, totally

dissipatable,
dissolvable in the dark-
true and liquid

presence of night.
Tree branches
swaying as though

through time,
its deficiencies,
mortality could

rise up and prick
his sleeve.
When he falls

he's embedded
in the snow.
The crucifixion

a conjugation
into his next, his
higher life—

## Realization

Exchange my life and for what?
Of all places, here, before the bitter

complication of sky? Dawn. Whites. Blues. These
narratives I'd absorb
if I could.

Some things do not arrive.
Be thankful.

The snow is a skin. Inside it,
violence and I—we go
our separate ways.

I'm no longer a child.
My soul is not up for grabs,
right?

Drift

Something with a clenched fist rising from a spiked field.

Something with a clenched fist, unknotting, giving up to openness.

There's a well to fill. There's for throwing, a red stone.

There's a well to throw the red stone into, to fill it.

There's a well & it's the outline of a husband.

There's a red stone to throw the outline of a husband into.

There's a red husband but you can't throw a well

into a well. The spiked field is hungry.

Throw the well between them into the spiked field.

The spiked field throws into the well the red stone.

The spiked field throws the red stone into itself. You

try practicing war solo, underneath—

x

## The Angel

There is an absence pouring a wind between us like a blue fence.

Grief

that rescues you.

Unspools you back into consciousness.

That head. Full of slush.

Bright premature traveler.

Dream me—

Good that you still dream.

Rescue

Then the clamped pitter-patter
          of paws rearranging the flakes, then
the paramedics
as if they were always
                    at hand, blares
of red-blue light rising, snow breaking, barking, the invisible
                              conductor commanding
                    the scene return like a score
to the outset, & his baton
                         is infinite, is
                         impartial, waving behind
the sky-blur
coming into focus,
          the freezing body restarting
          a symphony of warmth, the gloves
          grabbing & lifting, for a second
in the surround, the eye
          which has been frozen shut, peels
          open, & the trees begin to shake
          off the shower,
the dark becomes
a different type of dark, the blood resumes
          its work of searching
for openings into the world, light of van, no,
light of ambulance, no, of savior, of he
          whose will
          this can be only, & distance
                    vanishes
into yellow light, & knees settle
          inches from the face
                    & the vehicle starts

& the soul, having not been
        completely revived, attempts
        the cadenza, lingers
        its smoke in the imprint, in the outline
                        of your body
            that is already
      disappearing, melting, the dogs marching
through it, time hiding itself in the crescendos of snow,
                      finding the first note

## Cleanness

Opening the blinds, it's almost true, I wasn't meant to see
the two of them dressing. What came before I had seen
many times, many different versions: unsuspecting, private
brightnesses, those who noticed my looking and returned it.

You watch a man manipulate himself into a key enough times,
you start to believe every lock is an idea worth picking around in, worth
investigating for whom before it has opened its mystery of metal, the
   sheets jaundiced with fluid, holding the contours of their interiors.

Look. And why won't you?

## And

there were rules not guidelines regarding the drugs' administration

and the doors our bodies automatically opened

and oh if you got it wrong you lived but only if you got it wrong

and my granddad just passed away nothing to do with you

and beauty is neutral which says it *becomes* the problem

like discovering your talent is to make people laugh

and I'm not going to New York to fuck a nigga I can fuck at home

and the ghost we call culture rationed between us, hammered by gleam
   in the Frankensteined light—

the mean heart of the situation burning in hopes of purity,
   geometrically, leaving

its carbon feedback, its tar, enough to clog tenderness—was I meant to
   delete my longing? to delete

the context? now there's bird-chirp on the window encouraging the sun

to stay down a while longer. now agitation. the two of you share a cliff.

his jumping-over activates the rope around your waist.

it uncoils like poison. it will come, the pull's offer.

the pull's command. now worse than becoming someone you loved
   you become no one.

## On Nataliya Goncharova's "Gathering Firewood"

Their great coats protect them from nothing
but gravity. Hate to say it. They need firewood
to substitute for *touch-me-here*—outside, a windstorm

blowing a scythe through the trees, snow
shaken off onto the cottage roof in white
hazes, becoming celadon when it mints

the ground, the by-now-dead grass glazing over.
There is no humor here, however much
truth punctures, the field cannot be both landing point

and live. Of this the field has no choice—which is still
to have more than the men, looping among the wood
for which insentient growth will keep them warmest

for longest. They can see the furrowed strokes
of bark, like curtains, long-time has sheathed
around the helpless trunks. Pain, now, also, blaze

now; in the distance, an old woman
eyes them and hunches over as they return
to the cabin to document love in the iced paper

of the other's skin. Here, where they light
their tinder, combustion an infinite process toward
what? Freedom? Exhilaration? The blizzard

locking them in to desire's twisted, unsurpassable
queue, condensation dripping on the window
like music that cannot penetrate. Form does not

cure change. Change is a disease glimmering
invisibly; the moonset dropping its weight
on the far side of the exhausted sky, pulling

up scattered remains of daylight in the east.
That they are ever proximal constitutes
a miracle. All that we are: melt and drain.

## Story

He's after
the venereal present

can you not tell

he needs experience
to mean something
like in a novel

night having already
retrieved its fruitful hour

back
from the mind. His
anticipation, valenceless—

he whom the punctum
had already struck
and done away with,
his body

the photograph
he walked past
on his phone

## Uses of the Sky

I take you down in the way native to men of my background.
Your tiny future's history, like a Pollock
from behind, all over me; ecstatic the way *let*
and *stop* dispose their nuance, visionless, artists
at the beginning of a new form: Black
boy. White boy. Nothing, when desire is involved,
*has* to be wrong—How glad I am
we could never be painters.

## Strange Beach

It's an opinion
the stars are unspoilable,

arrayed, random
in the night sky, lifting
the plucked sunflowers' corpses
from where they gather—

marred
by death, even they shine.

Perhaps they shine because—look, look
how quickly they vacate
their positions.

You can see it in their faces, the sand
petaling redefinition
in the seams,

unlike the sheer
immaculate garments they'd become
if only they'd surrendered what served
to root them—

fidelity brought them here? Is that fair?
Or is the way their leaves ache,
calling the boy in
to the waves, simply
concern's restitution.

The living have already been simplified.
The sand is not sand but law.

On the forever-curling horizon, dark
becomes light-blue serrations, inferring time,
had we control of it, could submit, its fissures
subdividing the beach into its discrete
fecund elements. Where I walk

I leave no trail
because a thought with legs
is not a man.

Do you get it? You were deposited here
just as that assemblage of pebbles
one day mimics a rock.

One day.

No one can follow you here
not having to become something else.

## Crustacean

Running your hand through a stream, a little crustacean attaches itself to your fingertip.

It punctures you where perception stops and doesn't hurt. No yell, just little trove of delight to feel this life-form clinging to you.

Sometimes grief—many-petaled, in the reproductive season, hot— cowers, removes its shell, briefly, and you see it, too, is simply a case of misplaced vulnerability.

In its vibration, we, ourselves, are seen. To love what you cannot see or to see what you cannot love? Which is your problem?

What is at the precipice of naming has overstayed inside you, somersaulting in the late hours, the infinite skeletal choreography of the repressed. Its implosion, its tape.

Every face hides inside it the decision to live. At a hilltop, you knot your hands behind your back, not with a string, but with a mind.

The grass pelts your face as you roll down the hillside, the velocity of recklessness. The beautiful daisies trampled, being pushed down deeper, deeper on the pyramid of unfair composition.

## The Applebox

All manner of men, silhouetted, blocking, like
avenues of philosophy where the living must intervene (or at least
appear to), blocking the club-light's only fulfilment
                                        to show us
what we are, or, in our slowness, being only able
to capture where light has been, were—varnished wood,
one lightskin guy's arm around another, showing off
his catch (unclear who's caught)
                                        among the melanin-black
jealousies that fade in the damp ecstasy of sonorousness—sing
along if you have to; you, who is easier to upset
                                        than a box
of apples. The perimeter provides the ideal vantage point
to be danced toward, so the real men stand at the edge
to deconstruct, before touching, what might move them—

and what is it? Is it desire lengthening its vermilion tendons
to the ripping point's disarticulations? The currency of glances
passed around like an oneiric drug on its last decadent use.

Sweat: drips of soul leeched through the skin to prove simply,
at times, there's a soul at all
                                        to be lost. I lose myself
in the dancing, I lose. I win.

## Orchard

The hard thing is not watching him give away the oranges he's
   split into slices.

Leave me alone, nature,
alone, obedience. Terror
buried in the ink-white map. No sky-clot,
no light finally, birds.

Gravity thirsts—because I feel it. Leaf-crush.

Boots mute.

I inhabit his orchard, am ingrained. Like a perennial.

And who would die here;
who would say: *have more oranges, my darling, have more—*

## Routine

You should recognize me, the questionless
vista, a geography of borders declining.
Collapse. Instant shock. In decline,
I am drying sweat, call me: unfamiliar blister,
white-blood-cell party of rise and scar.
Expired ointment to treat. I am a feared life,
an unencumbered promise tracing
a gold nail down the spine.
A skylight, at the doctor's office, radiates
through an octagonal roof. What inquiry
do we die for? The ears of the mouth
are where? Think of sickness as a smaller life
trying to escape and take you prisoner
as courtesy. A friend is investigative, asks earnestly,
in her dog-voice, *What is it about England.*
Its thousand-year bell-ring, its bronze cast,
its ear-punch. I say, as if answers have ever
contained correctitude, *healthcare.* I mean
alpha and omega, the eternal promise-pact
of religion, the situation an unexamined lump
in the psyche. Are you malignant, born badly?
I'm an injury you woke up with, you saw coming.
My country a worn ligament. Hope. A money
I can't afford. Pray nimbly, as if we're given
nine lives. A child with an accent I wish
I could mute opens his mouth and his mother cares,
pills she's shaking in her expensive manicure. Little things.
Can they not be made perfect. The doctor, merchant
of minutes. How many bushels will keep me
in this dimension. How quick we find
our relation to disappearance.
She's good at her job of elongating. I hustle
the improvised monologue of my ailments in her

direction. She is the listening kind, hears flags in my voice—
I can't say I'm scared of dying. Will this rash go away
must be good enough.
She clicks a button on my existence.
*Lay on your side so I can glove the problem.*
If you get your hands in a thing, don't let go.
This is not the chorus of creation, keeping today
as one long tomorrow. Catch the flying song. What if anxiety
were a melody. Oh no. A rip in the sail

# Two Men Seen in the Window


Gunned lovers flinging their fleshy
scraps to-and-fro the uproarious
tremors of each    kiss exiting
via the cleanest    route the body
has to offer    (bowels
fresh of hours)    their names
when yelled    matter
like jokes    stuffed with time's
laugh    in the wrong
direction    Yearning's
water steadies    its thousand
eyeglasses    of forgetfulness
over where    the uncooled
sculpture    in his thorax
throbs    & unthrobs
the mind's sea    steams the feelings
sliding off    in the ashtray
of clothes    littered
like a plot    around the mattress
of draped    skeletons. He wants
the touch    in his voice's hand
to speak    to his skin's
skin. Love.    He wants
to become an I, to say: you
are a god, I am obsessed with surviving
the unconscious lecture of your body
but that    would be
an easy lie—lying is easy
splitting back    into the
familiar selves    like signatures
written    in the wrong hand:
the hard part they're intent to master

## Desert

Hollow carcass with sun cloaked over. Flies like ushers, bare
In their orders. As we approach, they scatter,

Given enough heartless shame to storm, to delete, to pick
Clean, this felicity to the sand, the remains, the ambiguous

Flesh—all this waiting and for what rapid climax? He and I,
The eating kind, drifters between dehydration and dumbness,

Alive enough to skim the dirt-salt of the other's skin, restless
Necessary rays of light bouncing back off the gallery of bone

Death has made of the nameless, soon-to-be proofless
Animal—we walk, despite our rages of hunger, on both

Sides of harm, searching for bottomless wells to drink from—
Think back. There was one, miles ago, but the sand—the sand

Is edgeless. We don't know where we're going so we go
Inward to nowhere. Our heads look to either side

Of a golden cactus, spiked, thriving, highlighted by the same
Sun, its weakening imperative, unimpressive commas, the shape

Our fallen bodies depress into this wilderness, this insanity
Of choice, or what, in the pale sun's intensifying vibrations,

Had all along seemed a choice—Incorporate. Absorb. Improvise:
What else do we demand of earth? Water evaporates out

Through our scalps. Flies anticipate. As if what rose
From their fearful bodies were not the lie of instinct. Is it true

Or has it, like most encounters with aftermath, with shudder,
Only been made to feel true? He grabs my hand

Because one of us must prolong the sentence. I will not
Bar survival in him. Above, a vulture flock encircling

Like high black notes on a stave. They are a song
Into which we extend our pulse quietly, quietly—

# Love

Two old men sit on opposite armchairs, their adventuring done, the older twiddling lit incense between his fingers. It's what we're told not to do that we do: don't play with fire, don't age, don't die, at least don't die alone—as if taking someone with you cushions the loss, the incense forming a pile on the carpet. The younger thinks, please be careful with your stick, but he's tired of parenting; he's already had a lawyer, doctor, a daughter who's an aerospace engineer specializing in thermodynamics. Does anyone know anything? The American in her likes experiments, questions; the Nigerian knows questions are distractions. The younger looks across at the older whose head is cocked backward in sleep, a hot air balloon of thoughts. First, he could choke on his tongue. Second, more urgent, what good are dreams? In the older's mind, he floats out to when he asked the younger to accompany him at this crucial turning point forever. Whether he said yes or no, the truth is, the point would still be crucial, turning and forever. When he wakes, he wails, tries to convince that he was not unconscious, that he heard everything, shifting, creaking, a gust of wind blowing out the incense—scent of bergamot and mandarin rind giving way to pure smoke. Of course, of course, the younger says, ignoring the presupposition altogether. And what did you bring back, my love, from oblivion? *I brought back a sticky note, smart-ass*, the older says, *Here. Our names are on it, yours above mine.*

## Mother Poetica

I write

because she can't write back

or because she won't write back,

or didn't, wouldn't. Men like me

play around her body

the way a cellist wrists a scale:

pizzicato. Permanent. Until

the frequencies of perfection

spur the ear via the jaw—I no longer

remember how it happened.

Different to never being told.

Forgetting stays

in the first place.

I wish listening harder now.

I wish we weren't our own

thousandth take

on classical tragedy.

Dream this: death

an option the mother

cannot choose

because the changes he would make

to his representation do not

as a whole, disappear, come back

with their microphones

of erasure, signaling

nothing is destroyed

or created. You are not factors

in a truth. Plot

loses itself in you

like a distressed flare.


This is real.

Come to the gates.

You are alive.

Are in danger.

This is the dark chipped-off region

desire went looking for.

It found you.

You were easy to find.

Clap for history.

Do not stop.

## There Are No Houses in the Future

You wake up, and laughing is
behind you, as
history refusing to stay remembered.

Selfishness. That's what I
touch you with,
to know, for once, value
inflates beyond possession of a thing—

These are the tiny disasters
undergoing their
last crystallizations no one
can alarm about.
The man I was
has since rescinded such asks—
We are not fools. We do not get
to be free. What we get
is to be here

## Now

Then we're on the shore again.
The stars, from this angle, wet and shining.

Hiss of the wind stirring above us
in a music, drowned mouths—

He slides his hand into my city

and in my city
his hand
is disappeared

## 27 Ars Poeticas

1.

The poet died. The speaker was happy.

2.

The poet died thus the speaker was happy.

3.

However the poet died the speaker was happy.
What happiness was the speaker could not decide for itself.

4.

It needed the poet dead.
The speaker wanted freedom
but settled for happiness as consolation.

5.

Having accepted the death of the poet
the speaker, who was now happy,
recognized there was nowhere further to go,
what was written by the poet before death
was its life. Change this late in the game
was simply self erasure.

6.

But if self-erasure isn't violence.

But if the speaker isn't happy
whether the poet is alive varies. A flash
in a dark room, of which the memory lasts brilliantly long.

7.

The poet's brain is armed
with meaning. The speaker,
dropping its shield, admits
whatever needs admittance.

The speaker's not a scapegoat
but they disappear
after too many shots.

But if self-erasure isn't violence,
the speaker isn't living.

8.

The speaker hasn't a family
but was born.
Only it knows where it comes from.

9.

The poet's death is a catalyst
for happiness. Whilst the poet is alive
the speaker cannot be celebrated.

10.

This doesn't hurt the speaker.

11.

Nothing ever hurts the speaker.

12.

The hurt speaks. The speaker
is a recurring attempt
to poorly listen.

13.

Take for example Clytemnestra
whispering, after death, about Orestes:
I do not *mean* to cause him harm.

14.

The speaker is an effort of pulling
in opposite directions. The speaker
cannot be canceled out
but it can say more than the poet intended.

15.

She is a ghost.
Her son is now free to define happiness.

16.

Mothers write their sons.
Upon death, this doesn't matter.

17.

Happiness matters.
The speaker can't define it.
Speaking defines it.

18.

The moment of dying is not the moment of death
though it is common to misconstrue this.

If the poet wasn't dying
where would the speaker come from?

19.

It's the dialectic of expression.
After an extended period of cold, burns.

20.

Cold is not real.

21.

Absence is real.

22.

The point is not to prolong dying (medicinal)
or to forget the vector toward which all life goes (optimal).

The poet cannot become the speaker
because the speaker is not living.

It's best to consider the poet as someone who's fallen
into a large body of water

and cannot swim. What happens
then. That's
the speaker.

23.

I don't mean adrenaline.

The speaker is not a latent superpower.

24.

I mean she does not mean
to cause him harm.

25.

What falls out of the pockets
of what she means and what happens
is love.

By that logic, love is the delta
between the poet's death
and the speaker's continuance.

26.

The poet knows not what continues.
The speaker continues the poet.

27.

The speaker can be happy about this.
The speaker can be happy
about anything it likes.

## Night on the Thames Path

To have settled in the fraternal space between play and fight.

To have, along the river, heard their names
  hovering in the head like an intellect of loss.

To have bequeathed each name to a seabird posturing
  in the black water they sprung from: his name for the coot,

his for the moorhen, his, the cormorant, the mute
  swan at last lifting off its majesty as if the river

were not its birthplace, were not where it watched you run

unevenly, run as if the mind could be abandoned behind.
  Like ambition; to have existed, to have loved, to have been

in your existing, your loving, rare
  the way a bone deep in the riverbed is still a part

of the assembling landscape as you step far above
  on the shore in the sand into a beige never-thereness—

All my beloveds. Somehow, it is *like* they were never there—

## Notes

"More Night" gains its title and refashions lines from John Ashbery's "Train Rising out of the Sea" from *Selected Poems*.

"Simulacrum" reworks a line from Natalie Diaz's "I, Minotaur" from *Postcolonial Love Poem*.

The first line of "Poem" is borrowed from Elliot Barnes-Worrell, who posted an Instagram Story displaying surprise at a flower that was blooming just before winter set in.

Throughout the collection I respond to a number of paintings by Edvard Munch and Dorothea Tanning, most notably *The Magic Flower Game* (1941) and *Sunflower Landscape* (1943) by Dorothea Tanning and *Dark Spruce Forest* (1899) and *Winter Night* (1900-1901) by Edvard Munch.

"The Applebox" was commissioned by the Royal Society of Literature for Dalloway Day, as a response to Virginia Woolf's *Mrs. Dalloway*. The poem reworks a line from *Love, Leda*, the posthumously published and only novel by poet Mark Hyatt.

"Orchard" proceeds from the energy of the chapter "The Orange" in Roland Barthes's *A Lover's Discourse*.

"Mother Poetica" reversions lines from Jorie Graham's "Le Manteau de Pascal."

"27 Ars Poeticas" borrows lines from Colm Tóibín's *House of Names*, where Clytemnestra's ghost beckons a guard to deliver instructions to her son Orestes. When the guard asks if Clytemnestra intends to cause Orestes harm, she says, "No, I do not mean to cause him harm."

## Acknowledgments

Thank you to the editors of the following magazines, journals, anthologies, and outlets where many of these poems appeared, often in slightly different versions than presented here: *Granta*, *The Guardian*, Ledbury Poetry Festival, *Oxford Poetry*, *Propel Magazine*, *Prairie Schooner*, Creative Future Awards 2022, *Queerlings*, *The Poetry Review*, *Runaways London*, *PN Review*, *Poetry London*, the Royal Society of Literature, *Southbank New Poets Collective Anthology 2021–2022*, and *Re•creation*.

Thank you to the various people who have, through my knowing them, provided an aesthetic education in lieu of formal study, as mentors working on the poems, as teachers whom I've had the pleasure of orbiting, as close readers, as friends: Fahad Al-Amoudi, Charles O. Anderson, Anthony Anaxagorou, Kayo Chingonyi, Harrison Clark, Will Harris, Adam Hebditch, Vanessa Kisuule, Sarah Howe, Jeremy Noel-Tod, Sandeep Parmar, Stav Poleg, Camille Ralphs, Andra Simons, Stephanie Sy-Quia, Lizzy Tan, Sam Williams, Karen McCarthy Woolf, and the 2021–2022 New Poets Collective.

Thank you to my agent Kirsty McLachlan, for your steadfast professionalism and belief in my work.

Thank you to my editors at both Soft Skull Press and Fitzcarraldo Editions—Mensah and Cecilia; Rachael and Jocly- for truly *seeing* my work and the subsequent, separate, yet mysteriously complementary editorial processes that pushed and grew me as a writer.

Thank you to all the people who make up Soft Skull Press and Fitzcarraldo Editions.

Thank you to the Arts Council England and Samuel Ross, who provided grants at critical times that helped develop this work.

Thank you to my mom, my sisters, and my brother—I love y'all.

OLUWASEUN (SEUN) OLAYIWOLA
is a poet, critic, choreographer, and performer
based in London. He has been published by
*The Guardian, The Georgia Review, The Poetry Re-
view, PN Review, Poetry London, Oxford Poetry,
The Telegraph, The Times Literary Supplement*, and
elsewhere. His choreographic work has been
presented at the Victoria and Albert Museum,
The Place, Central School of Ballet, and Studio
Voltaire. Olayiwola has an MFA in choreography
from the Trinity Laban Conservatoire of Music
and Dance, where he was a Fulbright Scholar in
2018–2019. He lectures in dance at the Kingston
School of Art and is a member of the inaugural
Rose Choreographic School at Sadler's Wells.